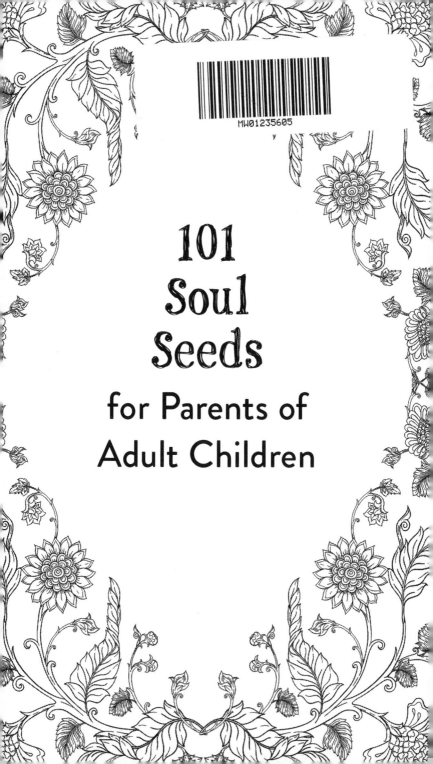

101
Soul
Seeds

for Parents of
Adult Children

ANAMCHARA BOOKS

Vestal, New York 13850

www.AnamcharaBooks.com

Paperback ISBN: 978-1-62524-778-0

Ebook ISBN: 978-1-62524-779-7

Cover design and interior layout by Micaela Grace.

Page border illustrations by Helenlane (Dreamstime.com).

101 Soul Seeds

for Parents of
Adult Children

Valerie Zehl

Introduction

Once we bathed slippery babies, then corralled adolescents, then watched as they graduated. At various points along that journey we might have exclaimed, "These are the best years!"—that is, when we weren't muttering, "Being this kid's parent just might kill me!"

And now we are parenting adult children, a whole new tightrope walk on a greased high wire.

Once they more or less listened to our directives, if for no better reason than we controlled the TV or car keys. Now they stand fully on their own able feet, and we hold nothing in the way of useful authority.

By virtue of maturity and experience, we probably know more about many things than they do. Does that mean they eagerly listen to our sage counsel? Maybe not. Can their unwillingness to listen bring up all kinds of roiling emotions in us? Oh, yeah.

The days of reminding our kids to floss are long gone, and such an admonishment would now be met with raised eyebrows or worse. We will always be their parents, but that doesn't mean we don't run the risk of offending or even alienating them now.

Good thing we love each other.

101 Soul Seeds for Parents of Adult Children is intended to be the last chapter in the parenting manual we all wish we had been given before we touched our first diaper. This little book offers perspective in practical pointers paired with

prayers and quotes to help us navigate this new tightrope—and reminds us that first and foremost, we and our adult kids are all souls doing our best to make our way in this world. They have their lives and we have ours, and when they intersect, it can be beautiful.

1.

We might say to our friends, "Thank you for being you"—but never say it to our children. Years ago we might have felt compelled to enforce the behavioral rules of the day's child-rearing strategies. But did we ever look hard at our kids and comment on their strengths? We can now. Now we can simply appreciate them the same way we appreciate the other beloveds in our life.

Spirit, remind us softly that they will always need us as loving cheerleaders—but no longer as the parents who gushed over their every achievement. Guide us to see them as the accomplished adults they are and choose our words and attitudes accordingly.

Affirming others isn't "flattering" them—
It's when you genuinely and consistently
acknowledge their efforts
and accomplishments,
both large and small. Make affirmation a habit
and watch what happens!

–LEON F. ELLIS

2.

When our little kids were within earshot, maybe we took care not to swear too brutally, criticize somebody, or demonstrate other behaviors we didn't want them to copy. It's no different now. Young or older, we're still their parents. Even if we can't see one another on a minute-by-minute basis, the energy we put out affects them—so for that reason among others, we want to be truly good people.

Spirit, You know our constant yearning to be better every day. Please let our children see that striving and choose to emulate it in their own lives.

When we strive to become better than we are, everything around us becomes better too.

—PAULO COELHO

3.

If somebody asked our children to identify our worst traits, what would they say? Their imagined answers give us good fodder for introspection—as well as potential for conversation and metamorphosis. As busy as their lives are and will continue to be, we don't want anything to make them dread spending time with us, even if it's just on the phone.

Spirit, please help us see ourselves as our children might see us, and then find new ways to serve them as their parents all the days of our lives. Please give us the right hearts to forego any egotism that could rise up in self-defense at their honesty.

My children keep me very
close to the ground
and very humble.

—WAYNE DYER

4.

Holding our children in our hearts isn't the same as having them constantly in our heads. How often have we lost ourselves in their problems, only to later realize that we were unconsciously trying to avoid dealing with our own "stuff"? As close as we might be, our children are still separate beings, with separate sets of challenges and paths to traverse. They will find their way—as we need to find ours.

Spirit, help us to remember that first and foremost, we are all souls. You hold our children in Your hand as safely and tenderly as You hold us.

You may give them your love
but not your thoughts,
For they have their own thoughts.
You may house their bodies but not their souls,
For their souls dwell in the house of tomorrow.

—KAHLIL GIBRAN

5.

In the introduction to *The Seven Habits of Highly Effective People,* author Steven Covey said he was giving his child pep talks when in fact he didn't believe his son could accomplish a particular task. What do we fundamentally believe about our children? Do we accurately perceive their strengths and abilities, as well as their challenges? And do we use that awareness to champion their growth all the time?

Spirit, please uncloud our eyes when it comes to seeing our children's essence. Remind us that they are Your kids, too, and that You endowed them with whatever talents they need to live their best lives.

Your kids require you most of all
to love them for who they are.

–BILL AYERS

6.

So many parents have issues with their adult children's significant others. "A man shall leave his mother, and a woman leave her home; they shall travel on to where the two shall be as one"; wise words from Scripture that can make parents feel as though they've been left in the dust.

Spirit, give us the humility to step aside to make room for someone who will be more important to our kids than we are. Help us see our children's significant others with Your eyesight. Remind us that every individual is a work in progress, no more imperfect than we are. May we be willing to shape ourselves to be positive parental influences in their lives—but only as they are ready to accept us in that role.

Do not judge, or you too will be judged.
For in the same way you judge others,
you will be judged, and with the measure you use,
it will be measured to you.

—MATTHEW 7:1–2

7.

When our children confront big challenges, they might suddenly drown us with phone calls or text messages. We do what we can to understand and guide—and might then be left with silence again. We could call and yell, "So what happened?!" but when they want to tell us, they will. Nagging them for updates might only discourage them from future interaction with us.

Spirit, help us remember that we are the steady outposts to which our children of any age can run when they need a hug or affirmation—and help us happily accept when they run back into their lives without a backward glance.

Humility and freedom go hand in hand.
Only a humble person can be free.

—JEFF WILSON

8.

Some experts say that emotional growth ends when alcoholism starts because drinking takes center stage in the person's life. Maybe that's true of becoming a parent too. Having children forces attention away from the parent's personal development. But when the kids are adults themselves, it's time to readjust. Time to look at our own soul and see how it still needs to blossom.

Spirit, help us remember that while we have many roles in life, none is more important than our identity as a soul. Guide us into quiet moments of contemplation and growth.

Personal growth is not a matter of learning new information but unlearning old limits.

—ALAN COHEN

9.

Our mouths can spout platitudes that worry is a big waste of time and energy, even as our brains coil endlessly around issues in our life or those of our children. We need to implement the wisdom we have read and heard over our lifetime and simply stop, and breathe—and pray—rather than pointlessly obsess.

Spirit, please stop us in our tracks when we get too wound up in the perceived problems of life—ours as well as our children's. You have demonstrated over and over that clouds can have silver linings, if only we can see them.

That the birds of worry and care
fly over your head,
this you cannot change,
but that they build nests in your hair,
this you can prevent.

—CHINESE PROVERB

10.

Author Anne Lamott has said that the most profound thing we can offer our children is our own healing. Amen to that. Of course we each have wounds to heal. Although we certainly didn't want our woundedness to affect our child-rearing, it might have. But it doesn't have to continue affecting us, or our relationship with our beloved children. We can do our best to heal those broken places.

Spirit, You know exactly where we are hurting, far better than we do ourselves. You've been called the Great Physician—so You're probably the Great Psychiatrist, too. Give us the toolbox we need, and the skills, sensitivity, and self-love to use it.

Even the smallest shift in perspective can bring about the greatest healing.

–JOSHUA KAI

11.

There is no guilt like that of realizing we made mistakes as parents. In our adult kids we might see the repercussions of the criticisms we levied at them when they were little—and now we cringe that we were less than perfect. If we had known better, we would have done better. We can use those words to help us forgive ourselves—and our own parents for any pain they might have caused.

Ah, Spirit, what imperfect specimens we humans are! Help us use the awareness of our own inadequacies to forgive our beloveds when they waffle-stomp our feelings with unkindness or negligence.

Forgiveness does not change the past,
but it does enlarge the future.

—PAUL BOOSE

12.

Sometimes we might catch ourselves in the most embarrassing emotion regarding our children—jealousy! Over the exciting new love, the great house, the huge paycheck. We need to step back and realize the blessing of our own life—and if it isn't what we want, then it falls to us to fix it rather than resenting our children for doing such a great job in crafting their own lives.

Spirit, remind us that in at least some small ways, our children's successes are ours, too, and that our joy for them should far over-shadow any pettiness that might momen-tarily rise to the fore.

You are jealous because you are unaware that everything you need is inside you.

—PETER DEUNOV

13.

Sometimes we might look at the human beings our children have become and wonder how much we are responsible. If they have challenges they can't overcome, did we fail to nurture their self-esteem? When they have successes, should we pat ourselves on the back just a little bit? No matter what, we can be thankful and hopeful always.

Spirit, our children are the inevitable product of our nurturing or any lack thereof—but they are so much more. We just planted the seeds. Help us be the very best parents we can be now, without bothering to look back with either regret or satisfaction.

Life is too short, time is too precious,
and the stakes are too high
to dwell on what might have been.

—HILLARY CLINTON

14.

Nothing challenges us as much as watching our adult children make what we might think are terrible decisions. If they don't ask, do we rush in to offer our opinions to save the day? Do we stew silently, waiting to sweep up the debris? Or do we acknowledge that despite what we believe, we may not hold the only answer to the problem at hand, and that we need to support them in their decision-making process no matter what?

Spirit, we might think we see gathering thunderhead clouds and want to put an umbrella over our beloved children's heads— but maybe we would then be getting in the way of necessary growth. You've got this, Spirit. Thanks for reminding us that You're the omnipotent one, not us.

One doesn't issue instructions to comets.
Grown children do what they have to do,
and parents can only grit their teeth
and watch and pray for them to get through it.

—LISA ALTHER

15.

It's said that what irritates us most about another person might actually be one of our own flaws. If the kids are 50 percent of each parent's DNA, maybe their worst traits came down from us. Perhaps in some happy cosmic way, we can help them by overcoming our own shortcomings. If nothing else, we can show them that growth is a life-long process with excellent prospects for success.

Spirit, open our eyes to our own sketchy parts and give us the energy to make them better.

It's not only children who grow.
Parents do too.
As much as we watch to see
what our children do with their lives,
they are watching us to see
what we do with ours.
I can't tell my children to reach for the sun.
All I can do is reach for it, myself.

—JOYCE MAYNARD

16.

No matter how long our children have been adults, the realization that they are now twenty-five or thirty-five or forty-five—ages we well remember when we were that old!—can come as a fresh shock. How often have we been guilty of not sufficiently respecting the wisdom they have accrued through life? Though they are younger than us, they may have some hard-fought wisdom that still eludes us.

Spirit, thank You for my children's skills, knowledge, and wisdom. Give me the humility to accept that they may know more than I on many subjects.

There is no respect for others
without humility in one's self.

—HENRI FREDERIC AMIEL

17.

When our kids suggest we try something different, or differently, our initial reaction might be, "No! I've always done it this way and that works just fine!" But taking them up on their proposal might broaden our horizons and show that we respect their opinions. Such interaction can also bring us one step closer to them.

Spirit, crack open the concrete of our entrenched thinking. We want to be malleable, open to new experiences and thoughts. Help us at least try whatever our children suggest, so they understand that we respect them as the intelligent people they are.

The mind is stretched
by a new idea or sensation,
and never shrinks back
to its former dimensions.

–OLIVER WENDELL HOLMES SR.

18.

What will our children be like when they are elderly? Will they be kindly folks who bring bread for birds in the park, or shut-ins who curse at talking heads on TV? We won't be around to see them, but we need to show them now what graceful aging looks like. We can whine about aches and neighbors or we can celebrate the beauty of life.

Spirit, help us choose to model a life culminating in satisfaction and thanksgiving rather than one shrouded by bitter regret. Remind us that our attitudes matter, not only for us as individuals but as quiet examples to our children.

The trick is to age honestly and gracefully
and make it look great,
so that everyone looks forward to it.

—EMMA THOMPSON

19.

As much as we might miss them, we need to remember that our adult kids are busy people. Unless we are in imminent distress, we should not be uppermost in their minds. We can stay in touch by sending silly memes, short texts, or even spontaneous presents, but whining because they haven't contacted us isn't good for anybody.

Spirit, thank You that our children are
invested in creating good lives. Bless them,
please, that they may constantly
grow in ways that serve You, the world,
and themselves.

When we manipulate others
to get what we want,
we often end up with empty hands.
Better to accept what others can offer.

—ERIN PENCE

20.

Companies formulate mission statements, and we can create personal ones—and encourage our adult kids to do so, too. Such little lighthouses can shine on our paths when we navigate life's inevitably dark hours. And every day, we can use our statement to keep us focused on becoming the people we want to be.

Thanks, Spirit, that we can keep on growing until we're pushing up daisies. Help us be an example to our kids of how to live life, not how to waste it.

The bigger your mission becomes,
the greater inspiration you will be given.

—RYUHO OKAWA

21.

When we are spinning in too-full portions of our life, we can be brusque and abrupt and inadvertently cause real damage to our relationships with our adult kids. We will always be their parents but they are not required by law to seek communion with us. We are capable of deliberately broadcasting only our best, and it serves all of us to remember to do so.

Spirit, empower us to slow down, to
think before we speak, and to use our
words to affirm our adult children rather
than criticize them.

To regret deeply is to live afresh.

—HENRY DAVID THOREAU

22.

Over the years, our kids may have heard snippets of their family history but never seemed to care very much. We might want to write it all down, though, so they have it when we're gone. They can then be witness to their immigrant ancestors' struggles, to their forbears' survival during the Depression, to the wounds incurred in serving during wartime. Those examples can fortify our children, and us, when we face hardship.

Spirit, every one of those ancestors contrib-
uted to making us and our children. Bless
each one of them, even those that have died,
and help us learn from both their good and
their less-than-great examples.

Our ancestors are an ever widening
circle of hope.

—TONI MORRISON

23.

We parents may have missed a golden opportunity in the months after our kids were born: quick surgeries to turn them into marionettes. Think how much easier the Terrible Twos would have been—and now, when we see them struggling, BOING! Up they go, bounding in the direction of brilliant choices. But alas. They're not marionettes any more than we are, and we sometimes only barely managed to survive some of our own really dumb decisions.

Thank You—we say guardedly—for the "gift" of free will. Frankly, it's not always the happy blessing You might have intended. We humans sometimes might appreciate being yanked in the right direction when we're not sure which way to go. Please consider this a formal request to gently propel us and all our loved ones toward good choices and away from bad ones.

Free will, though it makes evil possible,
is also the only thing that makes possible any
love or goodness or joy worth having.

—C.S. LEWIS

24.

In raising our kids, we could share only the implements in our natural and spiritual toolbox at the time. Our adult kids may have rejected our beliefs but, to our dismay, not yet replaced them with a better set. But we weren't always of soulful mindsets either. We can use our slightly-more-developed spiritual selves to shine as examples and pray powerfully for our kids in every dimension of their lives.

Spirit, it's not for us to judge anybody's soul journey, even our own or that of our children. We grew when we were ready to do so, and we can trust that they will as well.

Don't judge others for not knowing
what they don't know.
And don't judge yourself for not knowing
what life hadn't taught you yet.
People take time to learn.

—RICHARD MOORE

25.

In quiet moments, we can marvel at the exquisite architecture of something as ordinary as a sparrow at our bird feeder. With a few years behind us, we might have learned something about using time to its best advantage, to appreciate all life has to offer. Are our kids yet able to see beyond their workplace computer screens and daily scramble? If not, we can whisper the possibility into their ears.

Spirit, please hollow out our adult children's souls so they can be filled with the beauty around them. Don't let life's demands choke out their souls' cries to be in the sunshine of their Creator. Help them realize that life is fleeting—and give us patience that they will come to such realizations in their own good time.

Patience is the calm acceptance
that things can happen
in a different order than the one
you have in your mind.

—DAVID G. ALLEN

26.

When the kids fell hard on the playground, they came running so we could fix their injuries or take them for medical care. Kissing their boo-boos won't work anymore, and we can't force them to seek the help we might think they need. But our children have brains in their heads and they know how to use them, no matter what we might think about their apparent reluctance to do so occasionally.

Spirit, thanks for Your longsuffering in watching us stumble and fall over the same stone more than once. Please guide our children to find the appropriate resources and not feel bad about themselves for what they perceive to be their inadequacies.

Interdependence is and ought to be
as much the ideal as self-sufficiency.

—MAHATMA GANDHI

27.

Touching a hot stove was a lesson most kids didn't need to learn twice—but sometimes they might have made the same bad choices and experienced the same painful outcomes more than once because they were stubborn. That's not the only negative trait they inherited from us as parents, and it's not a permanent curse they can't overcome—particularly if we serve as good examples.

Spirit, when we get frustrated with our adult Mini-Me's, remind us that we made more than our own share of stubborn missteps. Turbo-charge their brains to learn more quickly than their parents did.

Mistakes are a part of being human.
Appreciate your mistakes for what they are:
precious life lessons that can
only be learned the hard way.

—AL FRANKEN

28.

Since they were born, our kids have watched us climb the ladder of life. They've watched us wrestle to pull ourselves up higher, then miss a step and scramble for a foothold. They may have gasped as we crashed to the ground in a crumpled heap—but they've never seen us stay down because even at this moment we can choose to rise from any failure.

Spirit, our beloved children will encounter their own set of successes and failures, too. Remind them that they are better than their worst moments and stronger than they know.

Failure is not falling down
but refusing to get up.

—CHINESE PROVERB

29.

When we see our adult kids get guarded expressions on their faces when we counter something they've just said, we can guess that they no longer feel free to tell us what they're really thinking. Is that the kind of relationship we want? If not, it falls to us to take cues from their reactions to help craft the communion we want with them.

Spirit, it's so easy to know what kind of relationships we want with our children but so hard to achieve it sometimes. Puncture our egos so we are not propelled by a need to be the smartest one in the room. It's their time to grow into that role, and it's our time to simply let our faces shine with pride so they can see it.

Humility will open more doors
than arrogance ever will.

—ZIG ZIGLER

30.

We can write down what we remember of our kids' childhoods—such as exploits in potty training, friends, and favorite toys—and then write about them as adolescents, teens, and young adults. In doing so, we can show them some aspects of themselves of which they may not be aware. Much later on, our kids can read our words when we're gone and know not only how we saw them, but how much we loved them.

Spirit, our love for our children has no bounds but sometimes being human gets in the way of expressing it. Give us the gift of being able to detail the beauty and strength we see in each of our children so they will be able to recognize those traits in themselves, too.

Love is a verb,
an act of the will as much as the heart,
which needs to be expressed
in countless ways,
in actions as well as words.

—RICHARD DUNHAM

31.

Our kids' intimate relationships create danger zones for caring parents. Side with the kid during an argument and we risk alienating the significant other who learns about it later. Or side with the significant other and, even if we're right, we jeopardize our standing with our adult child. What to do, what to do? How about weighing every word ten times before it leaves our lips—or don't say anything preachy at all?

Spirit, thank You for giving us a sense of humor for these not-so-fun patches of parenting adult children. Thanks for the reminder that their lives truly are their own. We can offer input—indeed, brilliance!—if we dare, but what they choose to do with it is entirely their choice. Remind us that our skyrocketing blood pressure might be an overreaction to what is possibly simply their vehement venting. They are capable; they can handle it.

A well-developed sense of humor is the pole
that adds balance to your steps
as you walk the tightrope of life.

–WILLIAM ARTHUR WARD

32.

No matter how much we might prefer otherwise, none of us is immortal. And not only will we certainly be leaving the planet someday, but it might be a messy exit. We can talk to our kids now about how we want our lives to unfold as we age. We can write our wills and health-care proxies and such, and tell them the whereabouts of our most important financial information. Most of all, we can remind them that we want to spend every possible moment that remains in close communion with the beautiful people that they have become.

Spirit, we want ours to be peaceful partings. Whether it happens five or fifty years from now, we don't want to leave a mess. Not emotionally, with unresolved issues, nor materially, with surprise bills or overstuffed closets. Help us be ready whenever You call—and help our adult kids be ready to grieve because of the huge love we share and then move on quickly and live their very best lives.

No one wants to die.
Even people who want to go to heaven
don't want to die to get there.
And yet, death is the destination we all share.
No one has ever escaped it, and that is how it should be,
because death is very likely the single best
invention of life. It's life's change agent.
It clears out the old to make way for the new.

—STEVE JOBS

33.

When kids were small, they often alternately loved or disliked their siblings. Sometimes they were best friends—until they weren't. Now they are adults, which means they have moved farther along their individual path, and even identical twins are very different people. They may not share the same opinion about politics or cooking. They might be staunch allies in times of trouble yet gripe about each other in everyday conversation. But they are siblings, we can remind them, and they should hold that unique relationship precious, no matter what.

Spirit, as family members our hearts and lives entwine. Please let those bonds be elastic enough to stretch but strong enough that they can never break, even when one or the other of us wants to bolt. As much as natural relationships matter, thanks for the reminder that we are an integral part of a much larger family—namely Yours.

Families are the compass that guide us.
They are the inspiration to reach great heights,
and our comfort when we occasionally falter.

—BRAD HENRY

34.

When life gets scary, it's human to want to reach out for hugs from loved ones. But we need to remember that our adult kids need to see us being strong, not weak and whiney, no matter what may be going on in our lives. We can ask for their emotional support, but beyond that—nope. We are the parental units, not them. They are not responsible for our unexpected bills, nor for restoring our equilibrium. We want to demonstrate self-sufficiency and graceful aging, so they will remember our examples when their time to be an old person comes.

Spirit, thank You for bringing children into our lives. Please help us always be the people we want to be, rather than allowing ourselves to be needy at our adult children's expense. When worries pile up, remind us that we are strong alone and downright invincible with Your help.

Worry does not empty tomorrow of its sorrow.
It empties today of its strength.

—CORRIE TEN BOOM

35.

We can drown our adult children in what we perceive to be really great presents, like all the garage sale items we just know they will love. But our sensibilities are not theirs (let alone their significant others'), and if they don't see the value in what we bring, then we risk imposing stuff—and by extension, ourselves—on them. What we thought were really cool positives can become foul negatives unless we remember to offer them gently and are prepared to graciously accept a "no thanks."

Ah, Spirit, remind us to curb our enthusiasms if they don't match what our adult children actually want from us. Let us instead learn to listen hard to what it is they really would appreciate (and then please show us that particular stuff at garage sales!).

The greatest gift you can give another
is the purity of your attention.

—RICHARD MOSS

36.

How often we forget that our kids are fully functioning adults now, with opinions shaped by years not spent under our roof. We can't see them as the impulsive seven-year-olds they once were, but as the (mostly!) judicious adults they have become. We need to meet them where they are, not where they once were. Failing to respect them can erode their self-esteem, not to mention their relationships with us.

Spirit, give us discernment to see who our adult children really are, and who they are striving to become. Help us remember to temper our opinions and give only the very softest of criticisms. You love and support us; help us do the same for our beloved children.

Respect is one of the
greatest expressions of love.

—MIGUEL ANGEL RUIZ

37.

"Empty nest syndrome" seems like an inappropriate and inaccurate term. Birds don't seem to have any problem moving on once their offspring have taken flight. Indeed, that's what those little wings are made for. Momma and papa birds don't seem to badger the kids about flying together next Sunday or remembering to keep in touch. Perhaps we can learn from the birds. Do we want our kids to visit because we nagged them into it? (Well, maybe . . . No!) We can be appreciative of whatever time they give us and find ways to optimize every split-second so they'll want to do it again—soon.

Spirit, we are whole within ourselves, but we don't always remember that. Time spent with our adult children is glitter sprinkled into our lives and we are thankful for it— but our lives are full and beautiful, no matter what.

Holding on is believing that there's only a past; letting go is knowing that there's a future.

—DAPHNE ROSE KINGMA

38.

Some Mother's Day cards say, "thank you for giving me life" but that sentiment might be a bit misplaced. Yes, the mother's womb was the workshop for developing babies, but she can hardly be credited for that initial spark of life. She did not create her kids the same way she would make a meatloaf. She had no input as to hair color or personality. That was all magic from a Force much bigger, which has never yet demanded that we pay any sort of homage for the gift of life. Having children was our biggest gift, ever.

Ah, Spirit, thank You for giving all of us life. For knowing each of us right down to the number of hairs on our heads. For knowing what we need and sliding both challenges and joy into our lives so we can all grow.

We have been given the gift of life
in this perplexing world
to become who we ultimately are:
creatures of boundless love,
caring compassion, and wisdom.

—WAYNE TEASDALE

39.

When we compare memories with those of our adult kids, the contrast can be astonishing—and revealing. Our different perspectives can remind us sharply that ours is not the only way of looking at things present or past. If a memory hurts them, we can kiss that emotional wound now and remind them that we were doing the best we could at the time and that we're sorry if we hurt them. How we choose to react to their painful memories will have an impact on shaping our future together, for good or ill.

Spirit, more than any other humans on earth, our kids know when we have been less than our best. Let us take their feelings into consideration rather than reacting with knee-jerk defensiveness when they tell us we could have done better. Whether we agree with their take on our history or not, we always want to give their feelings the respect they deserve.

So whenever that brittle voice of dissatisfaction
emerges within me, I can say
"Ah, my ego! There you are, old friend!"
It's the same thing when I'm being criticized
and I notice myself reaching
with outrage, heartache, or defensiveness.
It's just my ego, flaring up and testing its power.
In such circumstances, I have learned
to watch my heated emotions carefully,
but I try not to take them too seriously,
because I know that it's merely my ego
that has been wounded—never my soul.

—ELIZABETH GILBERT

40.

Families were shattered during the Civil War and that can happen now, too. Because our children shared our dinner table conversation for eighteen or so years doesn't mean they share our political views as adults. We can disagree, even debate, but we need to closely monitor the temperature of such discourse to be sure we focus our anger on injustice, incivility, and ugliness—rather than on each other.

Spirit, we never want to see anybody as anything less than Your children, no matter how outrageous we may think their political stance to be. Our relationships, particularly with our adult kids, mean far more to us than does "being right."

Confidence comes not from always being right but from not being afraid to be wrong.

—PETER MCINTYRE

41.

It has been said that if parents don't talk to their little ones' hearts when they're young, trying to do that when they're adults is difficult. We might not have had the time or sensitivity to achieve all we hoped in that regard, but it's never too late. We are all adults now, and all evolving. How we choose to grow will determine the degree of closeness we will share from now on.

Spirit, we sometimes repelled what You tried to put into our hearts, so of course our children might have done so with us, too. But it's not too late for us to grow in closeness to You and to our adult children.

You are never too old to set a new goal or to dream a new dream.

—C. S. LEWIS

42.

When we try to connect deeply with our adult kids but find that they're just not open to it, we need to remember that it's not "all about me." They have full lives. Their brains may be spinning around problems and concerns about which we are in the dark. Or maybe they're simply not feeling particularly touchy-feely when we're in the mood for a verbal or physical hug. Taking their reactions personally can't lead to anything positive. Forget it and move on!

Spirit, thank You that our kids love us, even when they're too preoccupied to show it. Help us be patient and understanding, and appreciative of whatever they can offer at any time.

Your child's life will
be filled with fresh experiences.
It's good if yours is as well.

—MARGARET RUTHERFORD

43.

When our adult kids are going through Really Big Stuff, it's all we can do to sleep and digest food. Their anguish can totally preoccupy us if we let it—but to what purpose? If indeed we can impact their lives by sending positive energy and prayers, then that's our job. If we can remind them that they are strong and wise and capable, that's a huge gift we can give them. And if we can point them toward their Creator without being overbearing, maybe that's our biggest role of all.

Spirit, our adult kids are Your children, too. It's foolish to think we care more about their well-being and growth than You do. Thanks for holding us all in a love we can never fathom, and for reminding us that You are so very much bigger and more powerful than we are.

Sometimes love means letting go
when you want to hold on tighter.

—MELISSA MARR

44.

We can look at our adult kids and see traces of both DNA sets. Strengths, yes, but a glaring bunch of weaknesses, too. We can point out our kids' flaws—if we want to risk instigating trouble—or we can model the overcoming of our own set of lesser traits and encourage their other parent to do the same. We can mention our progress in discussions with our kids, talking about our own struggle to be better people. They're smart enough to extrapolate and draw their own conclusions about the growth we hope to see in them.

Spirit, You know we all want to be the A-Number-One Best Parents Who Ever Lived, but so far we have not hit that benchmark. Show us where we lack and help us grow better every day so we can model the very best for our adult kids.

Growth must be chosen again and again.

—ABRAHAM MASLOW

45.

Are we perceptive of our adult kids' feelings about the hardships in their lives? Is life making them better—or bitter? We can gently guide them away from unproductive frames of mind. And what do they see when they watch us deal with our own times of trial? When we're dead and gone, what sort of person will they remember? We need to "show them how it's done," by being sure we live up to the standards we set for ourselves as human beings, no matter what may confront us.

Spirit, touch our adult kids' hearts that they can remain soft despite the harshness and hardness of life. Help us transcend all of life's inevitable trials with humor and grace—and most of all, a growing faith in You.

I will not cause pain
without allowing something
new to be born.

—ISAIAH 66:9

46.

When our adult children regale us with news that a breakup may be coming with their significant other, we should go on Red Alert to see the danger inherent in any reaction we might have. If we agree that blowing up the relationship with that terrible person is a good idea, we may have to eat those words later and even scramble to repair the relationship if we were quoted to that person. If we defend the relationship, we risk our children perceiving that we are trivializing their experience and hurt feelings. Best to remember that we have two ears and one mouth for good reason.

Spirit, help us learn to be sounding boards rather than wanting to go beat up anybody who hurts our children. Give us the wisdom to point out anything our kids may be overlooking and to present it with the utmost gentleness. Remind us at the appropriate moments that giving advice can backfire, and that our children have the wherewithal to solve their own relationship issues.

Letting go . . . allows others
to be responsible for themselves
and for us to take our hands off situations
that do not belong to us.

—MELODY BEATTIE

47.

When hard times come in our relationships with our adult children, it's easy to retreat into a shell of woundedness and wait for their heartfelt apologies. But such a childish reaction can allow days to stretch into weeks and far beyond, and emotional distance can grow and become the new normal. Is it worth the risk, just because we deserve the apology? Maybe we need to put our hurt feelings aside and focus instead on the love we have for our imperfect children—and the love they have for their imperfect parents.

Ah, Spirit, we deserve to be treated better than this! We are owed that apology! Help us be bigger than those thoughts, bigger than our egos, bigger than our hurt. Help us find a way to sidestep the ugliness between us and our adult children to avert any lasting damage to those precious, unique, and utterly sacred relationships.

Forgive, forget.
Bear with the faults of others
as you would have them bear with yours.

—PHILLIPS BROOKS

48.

Friends are sounding boards for each other. When our kids are flying high, we are inclined to use a lot of exclamation marks in our conversations, not so much to brag as out of sheer delight at the joy in their lives. But maybe we should direct that happy punctuation at the kids themselves, letting them know how very proud we are of their achievements, rather than risk irritating friends whose own kids might not be faring particularly well at that precise moment.

Spirit, thank You for the beloveds who populate our world. Please bless each and every one of them, and all of their loved ones. Help us always be a positive force in each and every life.

Legitimate pride
in one's children can all too easily
ring of arrogance in another's ear.
If you want to maintain your friendships,
cultivate not only humility but sensitivity.
Yours are not the only children
in the world deserving of praise.

—STEPHANIE HYDE

49.

Getting to know our adult children's significant others can be a challenge. If they had difficult relationships with their parents, we are starting out in the hole already. And if they're really close to their parents, is there any room for us? We may have made the mistake of barging in, assuming they have tastes and personalities like those of our offspring. Oops! Not necessarily so! But simple, full honesty really can be the best policy: "I'm sorry! I thought you would like this, but I see that maybe it's not right for your needs," or "I'm sorry! I didn't mean that the way it might have come out!" Humbling ourselves, even if we don't feel we were wrong, is seldom a bad idea.

Spirit, please bless all our relationships with love and humility that overrides any differences and misunderstandings. Help us see each person in our life for who they really are, rather than who we might preconceive them to be. And please bend their hearts toward us, that we might grow together into a strong extended family unit.

An apology is the super glue of life.
It can repair just about anything.

—LYNN JOHNSTON

50.

Creativity is a gift we can use to stay close to our adult children. One might enjoy doing the *New York Times* crossword—so we can get them a subscription. And when we are feeling triumphant over a particularly cool Scrabble word, we can text them a photo of it. We might be hundreds of miles apart physically but thanks to technology—and a wee tad of creativity—we can touch base with our adult kids in tiny ways all the time.

Spirit, thanks. Thanks for the opportunity to connect with our beloveds; thanks for the brainpower to figure out the technologies to make it happen. May our little dollops of love be always well received by their recipients.

Creativity doesn't wait for that perfect moment.
It fashions its own perfect moments
out of ordinary ones.

—BRUCE GARRABRANDT

51.

It serves us not to identify as Parent Who Deserves to Be Heard. "Because I said so" (always a sketchy response) isn't reason enough for our adult children to listen to our words of sage counsel. If we think we have good advice to offer, we can present all sides of it logically. Shooting advice from the hip might have worked once when issues were fairly inconsequential but not in the adult world. If we want their respect as a source of wisdom, we need to earn it.

Spirit, supply us with whatever wisdom we need to serve as ongoing sources of support and counsel for our adult kids. And maybe even help them to listen.

A wise parent humors
the desire for independent action,
so as to become the friend and adviser
when his absolute rule shall cease.

—ELIZABETH GASKELL

52.

Terror strikes deep in a parent's heart when an adult child is in crisis—not only because of the situation but the parent's utter powerlessness. Even if help can be rendered, it might not be accepted. Having to stand back and watch events agonizingly unfold is almost too much to bear sometimes. "What doesn't kill us makes us stronger" is a trite phrase that rings with profound truth. It is through adversity that we experience the most growth, and that is true for our beloved children, too.

Spirit, just when we think we will completely
crumble from heartbreak, we see the situations
Your other children must confront. Please
comfort and provide for those in refugee camps,
in war zones, in the throes of addiction—and
please take good care of our children and help
us all grow from every adversity we encounter.

Something very beautiful happens to people
when their world has fallen apart:
a humility, a nobility,
a higher intelligence emerges
at just the point when our knees hit the floor.

—MARIANNE WILLIAMSON

53.

When our adult children confide in us, they have chosen to share a sacred trust. They believe us to be worthy of their confidence, and it's vital that we never violate it. Yes, sharing some of life's tidbits with a trusted friend seems natural and safe—but if that person ever accidentally or intentionally betrays our confidence, the outcome could be a permanent wedge between us and our children. Nothing is worth that risk.

Spirit, thank You for the tight connection that allows our adult children to trust us with their secrets. Please strengthen our awareness of the power we hold to hurt them by our thoughtless words.

Set a guard, O Lord, over my mouth;
Keep watch over the door of my lips.

—PSALM 141:3

54.

It might hurt just a little bit that we are no longer the first person our kids call with exciting news. They once ran home, breathless, to deliver such information but now it's their significant others who hear it first, who get to make their birthday parties and buy their most perfect presents. That is how it should be, though. We are in the backseat now—but we are still in the car.

Spirit, thanks for our places in the lives of our adult children. Cleanse our hearts of begrudging our limited role, and grow the seeds of love we want to feel for that significant other as well as our beloved children.

Letting go does not mean
not caring about things.
It means caring about them
in a flexible and wise way.

—JACK KORNFIELD

55.

Making the transition to an empty nester is hard. Even as they were entering adulthood, our chicks swooped in and out of our familiar nest, so we could feed them and check on their well-being with regularity. Now they have their own nests, and it's not even our place to tidy up (or even comment on) messy straw.

Spirit, thanks that we were able to help Your chicks find their wings and fly. We know that's the natural order, but please set our hearts at peace to feel satisfaction and joy rather than sadness at the changes in our adult children's lives.

Some people believe holding on
and hanging in there
are signs of great strength.
However, there are times
when it takes much more strength
to know when to let go and then do it.

—ANN LANDERS

56.

Some people encapsulate the changes in their lives with adult children in one heart-tugging phrase: "What about me?" They're not sure where they fit in, what their new role is. They've never walked a tightrope before and now their trembling toes must navigate one where the stakes are unspeakably high: being a parent who helps without hovering, who augments rather than overshadows the adult kids' lives.

Spirit, we don't want to make any missteps.
Please help us be our Best Selves all the
time. But if we are less than perfect—which
just might happen once in a while—please
plant grace in all our hearts that we can
always grow closer together.

My grace is sufficient for you,
for My strength is made perfect in weakness.

—2 CORINTHIANS 12:9

57.

We have a secret weapon when we haven't seen our adult kids for a while: FOOD! We can prepare their favorite meals and ask when they'll be free to come eat it. Or we can bring it and meet halfway, if we live a reasonable distance apart. And if they're simply too far away, we can make a batch of brownies or cookies and ship that little bit of homemade love to them wherever they are. Where there's a will, there's a way to stay close to our beloved adult children.

Spirit, maybe You feel that same longing when we're too busy for You. Parenting an adult child teaches us a lot about Your loving heart. May we offer nourishment to our children, both physical and emotional, just as You nourish us.

Food is symbolic of love
when words are inadequate.

—ALAN D. WOLFELT

58.

Funny how often we need to reinvent and redefine ourselves in life. Maybe we sort of figured out who we were before we had kids. Then we became parents and much of that personal awareness was relegated to dim memory. Now, wham! The kids are grown and gone and it's time to look at ourselves again and figure out who we want to be "when we grow up." If we are not yet who we want to be, there's no time like the present to propel ourselves in those directions.

It's You and me, Spirit. From the alpha to the omega. You and me, You in me. Guide us to all grow into the best versions of ourselves as souls, as well as human beings living in community.

One can choose to go back toward safety
or forward toward growth.

—ABRAHAM MASLOW

59.

It can frustrate us when our adult kids brush off our efforts to be even a little bit necessary in their lives. But it serves us to remember that real success in raising kids might be defined as "no longer being needed" because they can fully take care of themselves. That was, after all, the goal in teaching them to clean their rooms, sort laundry, and make lasagna. So . . . yay? Yes, YAY! Job well done, fellow parental unit! Our adult kids are self-sufficient!

Ah, Spirit, ignore our whining and accept our
thanks that our kids are functional adults.
Thanks that our bonds run far deeper than
the filling of their superficial needs. Show us
when we can help and when we should admire
from a distance as they go about the business
and busyness of their lives.

Self-sufficiency is the greatest of all wealth.

—EPICURUS

60.

This parenting-adult-kids thing is a game we never learned in school and nobody told us the rules—so we keep breaking them and learning the hard way. But then, we had to figure out a lot about toddlers, adolescents, and—God help us—teenagers without any instruction, and we all more or less survived. We can do it, this adult-parenting thing, with humor and grace and asking for forgiveness even more often than absolutely necessary.

Spirit, You made us in Your image, so we trust that our brains and hearts are up to the challenges of dealing with adult children, as well as their significant others and maybe their children. Fine-tune our perceptivity so we can avoid stepping on any toes or tripping anybody with our sometimes-clumsy efforts to be helpful.

By three methods we may learn wisdom:
first, by reflection, which is noblest;
second, by imitation, which is easiest;
and third by experience, which is the bitterest.

—CONFUCIUS

61.

Maybe our children have chosen not to be parents, so we must content ourselves with grand-cats, -dogs or -chickens. Friends might try not to gush about their own human grands, but their abject adoration is clear—and a delight to behold. Such wee beloveds offer whole new minefields of possibility for overstepping bounds, though. Grandparents go through the same sort of mental and emotions contortions as they did when their children first left the nest. The stakes are even higher this time around. And the boundary lines need to be respected.

Spirit, help us all be mindful of respecting boundaries we may not even recognize. Please bind the ties of love ever closer, not to choke but to unite us as family that can never be dissolved.

Healthy boundaries are important, but you may be building a brick wall when a picket fence would do.

—AMY DICKINSON

62.

It takes only one Gender Reveal party to remind us that times have changed. Black-and-white TV's quintessential 1960s stay-at-home, apron-wearing moms are long gone now, and today's moms likely also have careers that occupy much of their time and energy while Dad changes the diapers. Our adult kids think far differently about life and gender roles than we probably did. They order paper towels off Amazon, rather than the copious coupon-clipping and store-hopping we might do. Maybe we have a lot to learn from them!

Spirit, to be alive means to grow. The world is morphing at warp speed around us. Replace our desire to stay the same as we were decades ago with the awareness that "new" can mean "fun," once it stops meaning "scary."

Step through new doors.
The majority of the time there's
something fantastic on the other side.

—OPRAH WINFREY

63.

If we are open to being reminded, for example, that the small device in our adult children's living room isn't named "Alexis"—and if we can share in their mirth at their correcting us—new technology can be a tool to bring us closer. Our kids or grandkids might seem okay with being called upon to set up . . . Bluemouth? Greentooth? . . . for our devices, but we must always remember that refusing to learn to do for ourselves is a negative that can burden them. We are capable of learning how to manipulate our cell phones, tablets, computers, and even smart TVs. After all, it took us only a couple years back in the day to figure out the TV remote!

Ah, Spirit, life was so simple with pots and spatulas, pencils and paper as our main tools in life. Help us to get over our fears and remind us not to impose on our beloveds. We are well-equipped to handle whatever life throws at us . . . maybe with the help of a tutor or two.

Unless you try to do something
beyond what you have already mastered,
you will never grow.

—RALPH WALDO EMERSON

64.

Sometimes the best gift we can give is sacrifice. When one set of adult kids needs somebody to watch their elderly dog so they can join their siblings, we can offer to be that caring dog-sitter. Obviously we would much prefer to be with our kids and their beloveds, all in one place at one time for a rare gathering—but it's not "all about me." They need to know each other as evolving adults, maybe best done in the absence of the elder generation. There is value in such an offering, whether or not they take us up on it.

Spirit, give us a servant's heart when it comes to our adult kids and their families. Show us ways we can help foster the closeness between them, and please make it endure long after we have passed on.

There is no such thing
as a simple act of compassion
or an inconsequential act of service.
Everything we do for another person
has infinite consequences.

—CAROLINE MYSS

65.

The fastest path to truly dangerous living is getting between our adult child and their significant other. They will inevitably have issues with one another. Either or both of them might enlist us as sounding boards, and most parents will feel the almost-irresistible impulse to take their child's side. At all costs, we can avoid riding the crest of that impulse. Listen, yes. Console, yes. But we must remember that sooner or later the issue will be resolved, and we don't want to be in the position of backtracking on some vile observation we made in the heat of battle.

Spirit, help us be a neutral Switzerland when the nations in our world battle one another. Let both sides feel they can come to us for support and a bit of judicious commentary. Help us avoid taking sides, even when one side might seem more right than the other. We want our love for both of those individuals to grow.

Taking sides in inconsequential battles
throws more fuel on the fire.
Judicious neutrality can help
to quench the flames.

—TABBY DALY

66.

"I don't feel safe with you" may be the most awful thing we can ever hear from any of our beloveds. It can indicate they feel judged and that in response they retreat from establishing a deeper relationship. If such a horror ever happens to us, we can have one quick, heartfelt answer at the ready: "I am terribly sorry. I did not, nor would I ever, do anything to be malicious. Dumb or naïve, maybe, but not purposefully hurtful. Now let's talk about what happened." Thus are communication lines established and fortified.

Spirit, relationships can be so hard to navigate! Help us be accountable to our words, even when we said them with the most innocent of intent. Let every problematic moment serve to create stronger and deeper bonds between us and our beloveds.

If you would be loved, love.

—BENJAMIN FRANKLIN

67.

The more anxious and needy we feel about the relationships we are creating with our adult children's significant others, the more we run the risk of them backing away. We need to approach them the same way we would a new friend: "Here I am. Let's get to know one another." Their idea of a perfect family may be a far cry from our own, and us pushing for instantaneous closeness could be a major deterrent to that ever happening. We need to let our relationship unfold organically, trusting that the love we share for the person we have in common will be the cement that binds us.

Spirit, we want to welcome this stranger into our sacred inner circle with an open heart and arms—but without scaring them off with the intensity of our desire to make our relationship a good one. Help us learn to listen more and talk less, avoiding the impulse to "sell myself" as this person's new best friend.

Respect is the basis
for any true relationship.

—EMMA WALTER

68.

Saddling our adult kids with guilt might work short-term, but that's not the tone we want to set for our evolving relationship. We don't want them to come visit because we badgered them into doing it. And if they genuinely don't want to—then we can seek to understand (and remedy) the reason why, or change our expectations to suit the new reality. We may not get what we want, but that's better than them giving it to us begrudgingly.

Spirit, we don't want to be demanding, needy parents. You have given us this portion of our lives so we can now grow in ways that may have nothing whatsoever to do with our offspring. Help us feel in our hearts that that's okay, and even good. Help us show our kids what it means to be a fully actualized human being, and a fully developing soul.

Letting go doesn't mean
that you don't care about someone anymore.
It's just realizing that the only person
you really have control over is yourself.

—DEBORAH REBER

69.

"Meet them where they are" is an expression I personally am only beginning to understand, thanks to my new son-in-law. He likes heavy metal music and I assumed I would have to love him despite that scary inclination. But when I watched a Five-Finger Death Punch video with him, we ended up talking about the social-justice issues it raised. Their music is not just raucous sounds, I learned. That's just how my ears interpreted it. And my son-in-law is a thoughtful man in ways I had not fully appreciated. We can all learn a lot by being open-minded to other points of view.

Spirit, help us not be stuck in our opinions and interpretations. Remind us that what might seem objectionable might in fact have high purpose. Let us be malleable to new thinking, and to meet all our beloveds "where they are."

Tolerance is the positive and
cordial effort to understand
another's beliefs, practices, and habits
without necessarily sharing or accepting them.

—JOSHUA LIEBMAN

70.

We might not have ever shot a gun—or wanted to—but maybe one of our beloveds wants to share that experience with us. We could insist on sharing tea and crumpets instead, but that can send the message, "We're doing things my way" and that's not how we want our relationships to unfold. So even if guns end up not being our cup of tea, we can focus on the other person's enjoyment and encourage their marksmanship to indicate that we understand those abilities to be important to them.

Spirit, thanks for this nascent willingness in our hearts to try new things simply because our beloveds value them. Help us to be always agreeable, never sticks-in-the-mud about whom they will roll their eyes and be thankful when we leave. Help us to have fun, to be friends as well as family.

The open heart tries new things.
The willingness to venture
beyond our comfort zones
is a form of love.

—STEVEN JAMES

71.

From childhood forward, our kids are seldom slouches when it comes to catching our nonverbal messages. They knew to expect correction when they saw our hands on our hips and our eyebrows raised. Now the dynamic has changed. If as guests in their home we run the faucet full blast when we are brushing our teeth or leave lights blazing when we exit a room, we are silently saying we don't respect their resources. They can read nonverbal cues better than ever now, so we need to be sure ours are positive and send appropriate messages.

Spirit, help us be of the right attitude so our body language matches our caring heart. Remind us that we are no longer the power people in our relationships with our adult children but that each relationship is a two-way street.

Respect is communicated
with body language, facial expressions,
and actions as much or more
than it is with words.

—STEPHANIE ROBERTS

72.

Who do our adult children want to be? What qualities are they nurturing in themselves? When one builds a great bonfire, it behooves us to express our genuine admiration and appreciation. When another sets aside donations for the thrift store, we can offer to schlep them there. If any of our beloveds are trying to lose weight, making them their favorite cookies is no longer an act of love but can be perceived as sabotage.

Spirit, let us see our adult children's aspirations and find ways to support them. Let us all have the strength and courage to defeat our lowest impulses and act on our best ones.

Encouragement must be unconditional,
based on the other's needs
more than our own opinions.

—DORIS BARNES

73.

Our kids' choice of friends may sometimes have surprised us when they were young, but maybe even more so now that they're adults. At first glance, some of them seem incongruent with who we know our kids to be. But that gives us a window into unseen places within them. What is it about these individuals that's magnetic to them? The friend who lives on the edges of convention—does he represent a longing in our child to have more freedom in her lifestyle? The friend who is all about living luxuriously—does that appeal to our child who has always been so frugal? It serves us to remember that in the same way we discovered new facets of ourselves as the years rolled on, our adult kids are, too.

Spirit, the options in life are endless but some take us toward being better people and others do not. Please help us all make conscious choices about the evolution of not only our bodies but especially our souls.

Spiritual growth is never a requirement. It is always a choice.

—RACHEL DEARBORN

74.

We probably have some powerful opinions on child-rearing, having made plenty of mistakes along the way. When we watch younger people handling their own children, we might cringe. How tough it must be to be a caring grandma and watch while little ones are disciplined too severely or not taught to say "please" and "thank you." But every one of us can use ourselves as quiet examples of how we feel things ought to be. More than one foster child, who went through life unloved and abused, points to one single individual whose compassion saved them. No matter how limited our roles in life, we can make a big difference in the life of a child.

Spirit, more than anything we want to be a positive force in the lives of our beloveds and of everybody in the world at large. Help us remember to dispense love at all times, not only to the innocent but to those we feel might be being overly harsh or unkind, knowing they might need our love most of all.

A grandparent's job isn't to criticize.
It's to love unconditionally.

—LOIS COBIN

75.

When adult children are caught up in life-and-death struggles with dark forces, watching can be a heart-stopping, paralyzing experience. We must remember that we have wrestled with our own demons and didn't always win those battles. Our children's stumbles, while excruciating to watch, may be more valuable than their more victorious steps. We trust that the best in all of us will ultimately prevail.

Spirit, how very much we want to be the best we can—and our struggling adult child undoubtedly feels the same way even when prostrate on the ground after a fall. Please let us all feel the power of Your hug when we may not feel we deserve it.

The phoenix must burn to emerge.

—JANET FITCH

76.

Most of us have "stuff" that deserves a place on a psychiatrist's couch. So of course our adult kids might, too. Some of it may well be the fault of imperfect parental units, but we weren't the only factors in our kids' lives. We did our best, which admittedly is not saying much when we were still figuring life out while presuming to raise small people. We might want to reveal to our kids that we have benefitted from therapy, that some of our friends have—and that they undoubtedly would, too.

Spirit, we both pat ourselves on the back and whack ourselves upside the head as we watch our adult children. Help us remember that our role was really only a part of their blossoming, for both good and not-great, and that their struggles will ultimately contribute to their strength of character.

As parents, it's a form
of arrogance to give ourselves
either too much credit or too much blame.
Our children are individuals
in their own right,
not mere byproducts of our parenting,
and they have made their own choices in life.

—DOROTHY BEARDSLEY

77.

It might come as a complete shock that one of our beloveds thinks the toilet paper should be dispensed upside down. What? Aren't some things simply wrong?? Apparently not, at least when it comes to toilet paper . . . and salting pasta water and hanging potholders near the stove . . . and other minutiae of life that we might have thought to be incontrovertible. Maybe that's the biggest danger: that we assume our way is the only way and we feel fully ready to dismiss other (non!)possibilities out of hand. How self-centered is that?

Spirit, we each have spent a lifetime trying not to be self-centered and yet—there it is! Evidence to the contrary, which we might have never once noticed before. Please sharpen our awareness and sensitivity to respect other ways of approaching all the little and big things in life.

We are set in our ways,
bound by our perspectives
and stuck in our thinking.

–JOEL OSTEEN

78.

In today's world where so many marriages or deep relationships dissolve, it's a wonder significant others ever allow their in-laws intimate entry into their hearts. They're taking a gamble if they let themselves love a new set of parental figures, because future acrimony may turn them into enemies. We can only let them come to us at whatever pace—and keeping whatever distance—they choose. We can feel sad about that, or we can pray about it and choose to appreciate whatever closeness they offer.

Spirit, these are not easy times for enduring relationships of any variety. Please strengthen the resolve of whatever commitments were made by our adult children, and show them how to navigate the inevitably difficult passages of their lives so they grow closer to each other, to us, and to You with every step.

Commitment is always a risk.

—DONALD BUCKLEY

79.

It's a new world where voicemails go unanswered, but texts get instant replies. We can grouse because nobody calls or we can see what our younger beloveds are posting on Facebook, Twitter, Instagram, or other social media. In short, we can play this new game of life their way or we can be miserable about them not playing our way. It's our choice!

Spirit, our heads spin from all the changes around us. We know we are capable of going with the flow if only we can stop fighting it, so please remind us that "resistance is futile"—but in good ways, because our adjusting means that we can stay close to even the most physically or emotionally distant of our beloveds.

The measure of intelligence
is the ability to change.

–ALBERT EINSTEIN

80.

There is nothing we would not do or give to our adult children—but the most valuable commodity of all sometimes eludes us: to sit in silence and pray. It seems really lame sometimes. "If only I could DO something to impact my child's situation," we think to ourselves, oblivious to the powerful tools at our disposal. So why don't we do it for hours at a time, and even more when our beloveds are struggling? Good question.

Spirit, we don't pretend to know everything about what "You" are. Cosmic energy, white-bearded Source, or Divine Mama—our brains are just too small to understand. But this we know: we can immerse ourselves in You and be a channel of that great power and love on the behalf of those we care about. In fact, we have no greater gift to give.

Prayer is the greater work.

—OSWALD CHAMBERS

81.

Otherwise intelligent parents might bring up grievances committed by their offspring decades ago—and then watch those now-adult children disconnect and move incrementally further away. It may well be that the grievances are valid, but so what? That any person made a hurtful mistake years ago does not warrant reminders today. Far better to celebrate achievements and moments that touched our hearts. Those are the only memories that nourish any of us.

Spirit, we could endlessly point out the shortcomings and historic missteps of every person around us—and our own list of missteps is painfully long. Help us forgive enough to forget, so we harbor only beautiful memories in our hearts about others—and ourselves.

Forgiving . . . creates a new way to remember. We change the memory of our past into a hope for our future.

—LEWIS SMEDES

82.

Maybe we still hold grudges against those who raised us. So what might be hiding in the secret chambers of our adult kids' hearts? Is there a way we can encourage our kids to vent, if they need to, about our words and actions that hurt them, even decades ago? We want them to know that we can take even their wrath, should they have it to discharge, if it leads to clearing out any lingering pain we might have caused.

Spirit, we want all lines to be open and clear between our adult kids and us. Help them to talk, if they need to, and help us refrain from knee-jerk defensive reactions. Touch their hearts so they deeply know that while we have never been perfect, our love for them is enormous.

We need to stop being afraid of anger.
Unexpressed, anger can lead to bitterness,
hatred, broken relationships,
and physical ailments.
Constructively expressed,
anger can lead to new closeness and growth.

—CAROL GREEN

83.

Some parents see their empty-nest years as anticlimactic, heralding the start of their slow slide into the grave. Because they are so entrenched in their roles as parents, they flounder painfully trying to get footing in their adult children's lives. But we are more. Bearing offspring is a necessary function for the sustenance of society, but "parent" is not the solitary definition of a person. This is our time now, to catch the edges of every frayed dream and weave it into whatever remains of our time on earth. This is sacred time. Time for "me."

Dear Spirit, help us step back and remember
who we wanted to be when we were young.
We are still that person inside. Guide us
toward new ways of serving and creating
and growing for what just might be the most
productive portion of our life.

Life is growth.
If we stop growing,
technically and spiritually,
we are as good as dead.

—MORIHEI UESHIBA

84.

Many of us don't have the luxury of adult kids living nearby, so we miss daily interactions—especially tough when grandkids arrive. We can't run to hug those little people when they're unhappy but we can read them stories using a video Internet connection. We can send them presents so they know we're thinking about them. We can listen to them tell us about their day, and help them understand what might perplex them. We might not be able to be there in person, but we can surely be there in heart.

Spirit, remind us that closeness isn't contingent on geography and proximity. It may grow best when we need to consciously seek it. Thank You for the loves in our lives, and help us appreciate them rather than feel sad about their physical distance.

Intimacy is not accidental.
It is maintained by conscious choices.

—KWAME ACHEBE

85.

We can't always help our adult kids when they have problems—but maybe that's a good thing. If children grow up in a bubble, never exposed to germs, their immune systems will be overwhelmed later. If our beloveds don't grapple with life's minor problems, they will not have the inner resources to handle the big ones. That grappling is tough to watch, but vital for their growth.

Spirit, please remind us that trying to solve our adult kids' problems isn't good for them. They have Your help close at hand all the time, and maybe big difficulties are what's needed to draw them closer to You.

If we're growing,
we're always going to be
out of our comfort zone.

—JOHN C. MAXWELL

86.

It's said that life is only as happy as one's saddest child, and that is painfully true. When one of our adult children is in the throes of serious challenge, it's hard to enjoy a single morsel of our life. But what good is being consumed like that? Praying, yes. Meditating, even fasting—yes and yes. But being immobilized with worry? Why? Doesn't that undermine our faith, both in God and in our child's ability to overcome adversity? We can also grow through our adult child's inevitable struggles, knowing that success—while possibly far away—is inevitable on some deep level.

Spirit, remind us that we cannot see the whole picture of our life or that of our beloveds. Even what appears to be earthly failure may count differently with You. Give us peace to know that, as Julian of Norwich so famously and faithfully intoned, all shall be well.

Granted, your separation from God
has caused you all this pain,
but all shall be well, and all shall be well,
and absolutely everything shall be well.

—JULIAN OF NORWICH

87.

Pain seeps from every pore of parents who have lost a child, and it's hard to imagine how they keep on breathing. Maybe faith brings the only possible comfort: the knowing that souls never die. Those who pass from the Earth may no longer be visible to human eyes but they live on in their most essential form, as will we all when our time comes. The realization that each of us truly is a soul having a human experience makes all the difference, even when that early experience unexpectedly ends.

Spirit, comfort those who've lost children. Help them draw closer to You and to the awareness that death is only an illusion that causes pain. Each beautiful soul lives on and on, forever.

Goodbyes are only for those
who love with their eyes.
Because for those who love with heart and soul
there is no such thing as separation.

—RUMI

88.

Some parents have evicted their children—even teenagers—as soon as they said they were gay. Such parents' egregious reactions are stark, but are we guilty of lesser infractions when it comes to our own kids? Did we ever dismiss their dreams as being impractical? Dissuade them from following their hearts in any way? It's not too late to see—and validate—exactly who our adult children are, and let them know we are proud of them for it.

Spirit, please pour abundant blessings on anybody who suffered for reasons they couldn't control, whether they are persecuted for their sexual identity or for some other aspect of themselves. Help all of us who might be quick to judge, even our own children—and especially shine a godly spotlight on erroneous thinking when it uses the Good Book to justify anything but love.

If tolerance, respect and equity
permeate family life,
they will translate into values
that shape societies, nations and the world.

—KOFI ANNAN

89.

We didn't try to fit size 10 kids into their old 6X clothes. In the same way, we need to stay aware that our adult kids are still growing inside, if not outside. Their take on spirituality may have changed since the days of wiggling in our church pew and eliciting their evolving thoughts can lead to some deep and fruitful conversations.

Dear Spirit, help us stay open to hearing our adult children's deepest thoughts without judging them if they are no longer like our own. Thank You that they are inclined toward pondering life's greatest mysteries, and please guide all of our thinking toward the Truth.

Give love and unconditional acceptance to
those you encounter,
and notice what happens.

—WAYNE DYER

90.

One grandma discovered that her beloved little one liked an orange drink called Sunny D, so she poured it into every glass at every visit for years—and years, long after the grandchild's tastes had changed. People grow in far more ways than evolving palates and it conveys respect when we ask them before we assume we know what and who they want at the dinner table, for example, and what type of clothing they might like as gifts.

Thanks, Spirit, for the opportunity to watch our children grow from being "Mini-Me's" into being their own people. Help us let go of our preconceived notions of how and who they should be, but rather let us respect them for their choices.

When you're finished changing,
you're finished.

—BENJAMIN FRANKLIN

91.

Our adult children may push in many diverse directions to discover their right paths. How often do we obsess over wild possibilities that never actually come to pass? It serves us to delay hyperventilation until decisions have actually been made and implemented. And even then, if our adult children make the choices we fear, life is not over. Decisions can be reversed but feeling that Dad or Mom withheld their support when it was needed can be a bitter pill that can stick in an adult child's throat for years.

Spirit, You watch us make all kinds of decisions You might not want but You never take away Your love. Help our love for our adult children cover them in whatever direction they may go.

Radical acceptance rests on
letting go of the illusion of control
and a willingness to notice and accept things
as they are right now, without judging.

—MARSHA M. LINEHAN

92.

Occasionally we might be on the receiving end of looks from our adult children that we can readily translate to mean, "Duh! I knew that." Ah, but we couldn't resist the impulse to put in those two cents of ours to "help," could we? It pays to remember that every such episode can erode their desire to hear what rare brilliance we might sometimes have to offer.

Spirit, knowing what to do isn't the same as doing it, and how often we fail that test. Please give us insight as to what is valuable communication and what might border on belittling—and to seal our lips rather than risk irritating our perfectly capable adult children.

The tongue of the wise brings healing.

—PROVERBS 12:18

93.

Being invited into our adult children's distant homes is no small blessing. They have crafted their own set of habits and protocols, evidenced when we misstep and they "correct" our action to the "proper" way of doing it. Tears can sting our eyes at the rebuff—but that's an invitation to discord between us. That adult child's ways have simply changed, and they want things their way—which intends no insult to us.

Ah, Spirit, help! Desensitize us when we feel hurt for no good reason. Remind us to demonstrate the pride we feel that our adult children have crafted beautiful lives that happen to be different from the ones they lived with us before.

Damaged egos are painful—
but wisdom may grow from the broken pieces.

—ABEL JOHNSON

94.

Our adult kids know us in ways nobody else does, so they are uniquely situated to help us grow—assuming we can take their observations as fodder for introspection rather than as assaults. When they lived under our roof, we undoubtedly pointed out ways they could improve. We didn't realize that old saw about children and parents reversing roles later in life meant that we might now be on the receiving end of their critiques. But so it might be sometimes, and we can be thankful we have the kind of adult-to-adult relationship that embraces such raw honesty.

Spirit, thank You for the level of communication between us and our adult children, even if we're not always delighted with what their words convey. Help us always choose to think hard about what they've said, rather than dismiss it because we don't want it to be true.

Nourishing are the wounds from a loved one.

—PROVERBS 27:6

95.

Many of us have hot buttons that can turn us from smiling to sneering in five seconds flat, and so might our adult kids. Theoretically, we have the maturity to diffuse our irritation. Our adult kids may not have gotten to that point yet and may react viscerally if we accidentally push one of their buttons. That's where forgiveness comes in—*must* come in, in fact. But it's not always easy to turn a stinging cheek, when our own child is the source of the pain.

Spirit, remind us that we are all only human.
Surely our adult kids have had to forgive
us plenty of times since their birth, and we
pray that we will go on forgiving one another
for the rest of our days.

Forgive us our offenses,
as we forgive those who have offended us.

—MATTHEW 6:12

96.

We can deal with our own aging body but its limitations may take our adult kids by surprise. They can grasp physical changes but we see the hurt in their eyes when our forgetful brain seemingly ignores something they've told us. Now more than ever, honesty truly is the best policy. We can apologize. We can write ourselves notes. And we can try to laugh if they joke about our near-future home in the Dementia Unit.

Spirit, we won't try to tell You that we're not scared, not only about aging but about its implications for our beloveds. Help us handle it all with grace, and to learn ever more to lean on You as our main Source of strength.

Even to your old age and gray hairs,
I will sustain you.
I have made you and I will carry you.

—ISAIAH 46:4

97.

Bad things happen to good people. It's a simple, painful fact of life. But when one of our beloveds suffers a terrible blow, it staggers us, too. We may never be able to understand why it happened, but we can choose to take the highest possible road of faith and strength in dealing with it to be an encouraging example.

Spirit, You have chosen not to give us magic wands or crystal balls, but You have made Yourself endlessly available to us throughout the myriad complexities we encounter. Thank You for these opportunities to grow closer to You, because that's really the most important thing in any of our lives.

Prayer does not change God
but it changes the one who prays.

—SOREN KIERKEGAARD

98.

Nothing is quite so scary as fearing we've alienated our adult kids through an argument. Pain is palpable—and so is anger. What we might not realize is that while we may be right, we might also then be alone. Being the first to apologize makes us the bigger person, and who should be the adult in the room more than the parent?

Spirit, again we come to You about ego.
It's not easy to ask for forgiveness when we
know we're not the one at fault. But doing
so can restore harmony and connection, and
You have shown us over and over how essential those are in life.

It is never about me being right
and you being wrong.
It is always about listening
with respect to another's opinion.

—JANICE MANGER

99.

Grandchildren are a joy. They have the potential to tie our hearts even more closely to our adult children's. Unfortunately, when it comes to grandparenting, our advice, possessiveness, and smug certainty that we know best can damage our relationship with those beloved children's parents.

Spirit, remind us that although we have years of experience at parenting, our children are now the experts when it comes to their own children. May we give our heart wholly to our grandchildren—while having the humility to keep our mouth shut about how they should be raised.

Everyone needs to have access both to grandparents and grandchildren
in order to be a full human being

—MARGARET MEAD

100.

The daughter follows recipes to the letter. The mother might have tried to do that once, ever. Put the two of them together in the daughter's kitchen, and Mom better adjust her cooking style, at least for that interaction. We can grouse that our adult kids are not capitalizing on our culinary creativity or adopting the hard-fought skills we offer—or we can delight in watching their meticulous attention to measuring-spoon accuracy and other protocols that are foreign to us.

Dear Spirit, it boggles our minds sometimes how different our adult kids are from us until we remember that even our best talents are not the Gold Standard for all people. Please never let our ego cloud our eyesight when we're looking at our beautiful beloveds.

Humility is not thinking less of yourself,
it's thinking of yourself less.

—C. S. LEWIS

101.

Money is tricky stuff. When we see our adult offspring struggle to make ends meet, there's a huge prompting to jump in—but that can inadvertently teach them that they are incapable of meeting their own needs. We won't be around forever, and even if we are able to leave them some money, they need to know how to manage it and live within their means.

Spirit, bless our adult kids with opportunities to create happy lives. Bless their resourcefulness; bless their willingness to work. Bless them in every way, all day, every day. And thank You from the bottom of our hearts.

The best legacy you can leave your children
is that of love, joy, and hope.

—APRIL KENNEDY

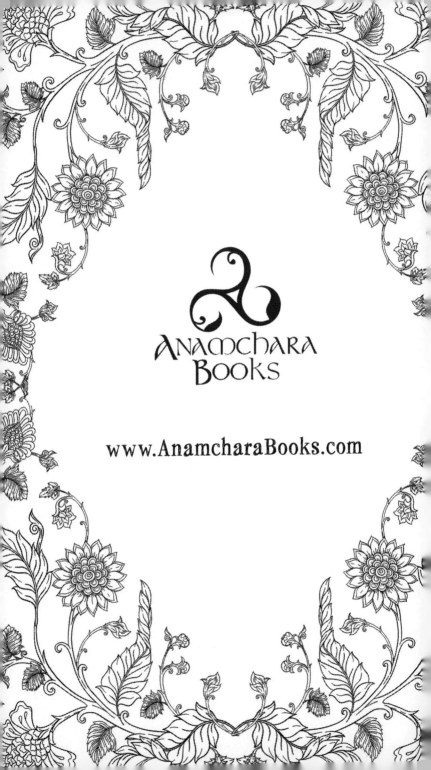

Anamchara Books

www.AnamcharaBooks.com

Made in the USA
Monee, IL
23 November 2022

18226845R10125